TASTY FRUIT

By NADIA HIGGINS
Illustrations by CHRIS BIGGIN
Music by DREW TEMPERANTE

CANTATA
LEARNING

WWW.CANTATALEARNING.COM

CANTATA
LEARNING

Published by Cantata Learning
1710 Roe Crest Drive
North Mankato, MN 56003
www.cantatalearning.com

Copyright © 2017 Cantata Learning

A note to educators and librarians from the publisher: Cantata Learning has provided the following data to assist in book processing and suggested use of Cantata Learning product.

Publisher's Cataloging-in-Publication Data
Prepared by Librarian Consultant: Ann-Marie Begnaud
Library of Congress Control Number: 2016938079
     Tasty Fruit
     Series: My First Science Songs
     By Nadia Higgins
     Illustrations by Chris Biggin
     Music by Drew Temperante
     Summary: Learn how fruits help plants spread their seeds and also provide us with tasty treats in this illustrated story set to music.
     ISBN: 978-1-63290-789-9 (library binding/CD)
Suggested Dewey and Subject Headings:
     Dewey: E 575.67
     LCSH Subject Headings: Fruit – Juvenile literature. | Fruit – Songs and music – Texts. | Fruit – Juvenile sound recordings.
     Sears Subject Headings: Fruit. | School songbooks. | Children's songs. | Popular music.
     BISAC Subject Headings: JUVENILE NONFICTION / Science & Nature / Flowers & Plants. | JUVENILE NONFICTION / Music / Songbooks. | JUVENILE NONFICTION / Science & Nature / Botany.

Book design and art direction: Tim Palin Creative
Editorial direction: Flat Sole Studio
Music direction: Elizabeth Draper
Music written and produced by Drew Temperante

Printed in the United States of America in North Mankato, Minnesota.
122016   0339CGS17

ACCESS THE MUSIC!
SCAN CODE WITH MOBILE APP
CANTATALEARNING.COM

TIPS TO SUPPORT LITERACY AT HOME

WHY READING AND SINGING WITH YOUR CHILD IS SO IMPORTANT

Daily reading with your child leads to increased academic achievement. Music and songs, specifically rhyming songs, are a fun and easy way to build early literacy and language development. Music skills correlate significantly with both phonological awareness and reading development. Singing helps build vocabulary and speech development. And reading and appreciating music together is a wonderful way to strengthen your relationship.

READ AND SING EVERY DAY!

TIPS FOR USING CANTATA LEARNING BOOKS AND SONGS DURING YOUR DAILY STORY TIME

1. As you sing and read, point out the different words on the page that rhyme. Suggest other words that rhyme.

2. Memorize simple rhymes such as Itsy Bitsy Spider and sing them together. This encourages comprehension skills and early literacy skills.

3. Use the questions in the back of each book to guide your singing and storytelling.

4. Read the included sheet music with your child while you listen to the song. How do the music notes correlate to the words of the song?

5. Sing along on the go and at home. Access music by scanning the QR code on each Cantata book, or by using the included CD. You can also stream or download the music for free to your computer, smartphone, or mobile device.

Devoting time to daily reading shows that you are available for your child. Together, you are building language, literacy, and listening skills.

Have fun reading and singing!

Do you like to eat bananas for breakfast or apple slices for a snack? How about a salad with cucumbers and tomatoes? These are all fruits, and eating them helps us to grow. But did you know that fruits help plants grow, too?

To learn more about tasty fruit, turn the page and sing along!

One, two, three, four, five, six!

Six plant parts and they go like this:

roots, stems, leaves,

flowers, fruit, and seeds!

seed

flower

fruit

leaf

Stem

root

Each part plays a special role.
Fruit helps plants grow and grow.

Fruit so juicy, fruit so sweet,
fruit so **crisp**, it's good to eat.

Peel a fruit. Bite under the skin.
Tasty fruits hold seeds within.

Fruits are tasty. It's part of the plan
to spread seeds as far as they can.

Animals come and eat the fruit.
Then seeds come out when animals poop.

Fruit so juicy, fruit so sweet,
fruit so crisp, it's good to eat.

Peel a fruit. Bite under the skin.
Tasty fruits hold seeds within.

Get up and move. Make a fruit **smoothie**.
Put in apples and pears, oh, so groovy!

Get up and move. Make a fruit smoothie.
Squeeze in lemons and limes, oh, so groovy!

Get up and move. Make a fruit smoothie.
Add strawberries and melon, oh, so groovy!

Get up and move. Make a fruit smoothie.
Peel bananas and **kiwi**, oh, so groovy!

Fruit so juicy, fruit so sweet,
fruit so crisp, it's good to eat.

Peel a fruit. Bite under the skin.
Tasty fruits hold seeds within.

Is it a fruit? No need to guess.
Can you find seeds? Then, that's a yes!
Cucumbers, squash, and string beans, too,
and lots of veggies are really fruit.

Tomato

Peach

Cucumber

Pumpkin

Fruit so juicy, fruit so sweet,
fruit so crisp, it's good to eat.

Peel a fruit. Bite under the skin.
Tasty fruits hold seeds within.

PEACH

21

SONG LYRICS
Tasty Fruit

One, two, three, four, five, six!
Six plant parts and they go like this:
roots, stems, leaves,
flowers, fruit, and seeds!

Each part plays a special role.
Fruit helps plants grow and grow.

Fruit so juicy, fruit so sweet,
fruit so crisp, it's good to eat.
Peel a fruit. Bite under the skin.
Tasty fruits hold seeds within.

Fruits are tasty. It's part of the plan
to spread seeds as far as they can.
Animals come and eat the fruit.
Then seeds come out when animals poop.

Fruit so juicy, fruit so sweet,
fruit so crisp, it's good to eat.
Peel a fruit. Bite under the skin.
Tasty fruits hold seeds within.

Get up and move. Make a fruit smoothie.
Put in apples and pears, oh, so groovy!
Get up and move. Make a fruit smoothie.
Squeeze in lemons and limes, oh, so groovy!

Get up and move. Make a fruit smoothie.
Add strawberries and melon, oh, so groovy!
Get up and move. Make a fruit smoothie.
Peel bananas and kiwi, oh, so groovy!

Fruit so juicy, fruit so sweet,
fruit so crisp, it's good to eat.
Peel a fruit. Bite under the skin.
Tasty fruits hold seeds within.

Is it a fruit? No need to guess.
Can you find seeds? Then, that's a yes!
Cucumbers, squash, and string beans, too,
and lots of veggies are really fruit.

Fruit so juicy, fruit so sweet,
fruit so crisp, it's good to eat.
Peel a fruit. Bite under the skin.
Tasty fruits hold seeds within.

Tasty Fruit

Calypso/Hip Hop\nDrew Temperante

Intro

One, two, three, four, five, six! Six plant parts and they go like this: roots, stems, leaves, flow-ers, fruit, and seeds!

Each part plays a spe-cial role. Fruit helps plants grow and grow.

Chorus

Fruit so juic-y, fruit so sweet, fruit so crisp, it's good to eat. Peel a fruit. Bite un-der the skin. Tast-y fruits hold seeds with-in.

Verse

1. Fruits are tast-y. It's part of the plan to spread seeds as far as they can. An-i-mals come and eat the fruit. Then seeds come out when an-i-mals poop.

Chorus

Bridge

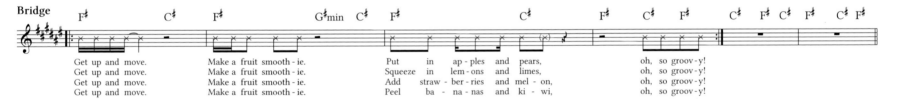

Get up and move.	Make a fruit smooth-ie.	Put in ap-ples and pears,	oh, so groov-y!
Get up and move.	Make a fruit smooth-ie.	Squeeze in lem-ons and limes,	oh, so groov-y!
Get up and move.	Make a fruit smooth-ie.	Add straw-ber-ries and mel-on,	oh, so groov-y!
Get up and move.	Make a fruit smooth-ie.	Peel ba-na-nas and ki-wi,	oh, so groov-y!

Chorus

Verse 2
Is it a fruit? No need to guess.
Can you find seeds? Then, that's a yes!
Cucumbers, squash, and string beans, too,
and lots of veggies are really fruit.

Outro

Fruit so juic-y, fruit so sweet, fruit so crisp, it's good to eat. Peel a fruit. Bite un-der the skin. Tast-y fruits hold seeds with-in.

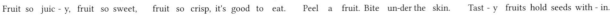

ACCESS THE MUSIC!\n\nSCAN CODE WITH MOBILE APP\n\nCANTATALEARNING.COM

23

GLOSSARY

crisp—firm and crunchy

kiwi—a small, round fruit that has a fuzzy brown skin and is green on the inside

smoothie—a creamy drink made of fruit blended with milk, yogurt, or juice

GUIDED READING ACTIVITIES

1. What is your favorite fruit to eat? Draw a picture of it.

2. Have you eaten any fruit today? What did you have? What kinds of fruit did you eat yesterday?

3. With an adult, cut open a piece of fruit. Can you find any seeds inside? Now eat the fruit!

4. Can you remember all the fruits that were sung about in this book? List them on a sheet of paper.

TO LEARN MORE

Aboff, Marcie. *The Fantastic Fruit Group*. North Mankato, MN: Capstone, 2012.

Bishop, Celeste. *Why Do Plants Have Fruits?* New York: PowerKids Press, 2016.

Gibbons, Gail. *The Fruits We Eat*. New York: Holiday House, 2015.

Hansen, Grace. *Fruits*. Minneapolis: Abdo Kids, 2016.